Arts & Crafts

BATIK AND TIE-DYE

Susie O'Reilly

With photographs by Zul Mukhida

Wayland

Titles in this series

BATIK AND TIE-DYE
BLOCK PRINTING
MODELLING
PAPER MAKING
STENCILLING
WEAVING

Frontispiece *A piece of tie-dyed cotton from Sierra Leone, West Africa.*

© Copyright 1993 Wayland (Publishers) Ltd

First published in 1993 by
Wayland (Publishers) Ltd
61 Western Road, Hove
East Sussex BN3 1JD, England

Editor: Anna Girling
Designer: Jean Wheeler

British Library Cataloguing in Publication Data
O'Reilly, Susie
Batik and Tie-dye.–(Arts & Crafts Series)
I. Title II. Series
746.6
ISBN 0 7502 0681 0

Typeset by Dorchester Typesetting Group Ltd, Dorchester, Dorset, England
Printed and bound by Lego, Italy

CONTENTS

Words printed in **bold** appear in the glossary.

GETTING STARTED

Bright sunlight and smoke change the colour of things they come into contact with. Have you noticed the patterns made when things are partly protected from light or smoke? Perhaps people long ago noticed these effects. They developed the idea of making patterned **fabric** by protecting certain areas of it from being coloured by **dyes**. This is called **resist** dyeing. Resist-dyed **textiles** have been made in many parts of the world for hundreds of years.

These designs ▶ *were inspired by the artist's knowledge of traditional batik.*

▼ *People in Africa wear clothes made from tie-dyed and batik fabrics.*

In tie-dye, the fabric is folded, tied or stitched. In batik, melted wax, flour paste, rice **starch**, clay – or whatever is most easily available – is applied to the fabric. Both these methods protect parts of the fabric from being coloured by dye.

The peoples of the world who have a **tradition** of making resist-dyed fabrics value them highly. They are worn by rich and important people and at special events such as weddings and funerals.

People from many developing countries still make and wear resist-dyed textiles, using methods handed down over the years through their families. Artists, craftspeople and **designers** from other parts of the world find these traditional **techniques**, and use of colour and patterns, an exciting source of ideas for their own work.

This book will help you to explore some of the many possibilities of batik and tie-dye for yourself.

◀ *Here are some ideas for things you can make: a patchwork quilt, a cushion, or a picture.*

Safety
Always make sure you have a fire blanket, fire-extinguisher or bucket of sand nearby in case of fire. Always make sure your hair is tied back and sleeves rolled up when using heating equipment.

SETTING UP YOUR WORK AREA

You will need to collect together these tools and materials to get started.

Fabric
Choose squares (about 25 or 30 cm square) or rectangles (about 15 cm by 30 cm) of plain white or beige fabric. Cotton and other natural fabrics, such as silk, work well. Artificial fibres, such as polyester, are not suitable.

General equipment
Old newspapers (to protect work surfaces, floors etc)

Overalls, rubber gloves
Drying rack (e.g. a string tied between two chairs)
Kettle
Plastic bowls
Cold-water dyes (e.g. Dylon cold-water dyes)
Salt
Wooden spoons
Iron
Sewing needles, pins, thread and scissors
Drawing pad and pencils

For batik
Wooden frame (smaller than the pieces of fabric)
Electric or gas ring

Old saucepan and tin can (without sharp edges)
Batik wax (from a craft shop)
Household candles
Wax crayons
Food dyes
Egg poacher
Stiff-haired brushes
Household painting brushes (1.5–2 cm thick)
Old screwdrivers, knives, forks for scraping off wax
Drawing pins or staples

For tie-dye
Thin string
Pebbles or dried peas

BATIK AROUND THE WORLD

It is not known exactly when or where people started making batik-patterned cloths. **Archaeologists** have found evidence of batik in the Far East, the Middle East, Central Asia and India. They have uncovered scraps of ancient batik cloth, and paintings and sculptures showing people wearing what seem to be batik fabrics. Batik is still made all over the world. Some methods result in big, bold, powerful designs. Others give delicate, finely-detailed patterns.

In Indonesia, batiks have fine, delicate lines and carefully placed dots. The wax is skilfully dribbled on to the cloth using a special tool, called a **tjanting**, which gives crisp, controlled patterns.

▲ *Delicately patterned cloth from Bali, Indonesia.*

◄ *An Indonesian craftsperson using a* tjanting.

Some Indonesian batik-makers choose to use **brittle** waxes which crack and allow the dye to seep into the cloth. Others prefer to use a more **flexible** wax, which does not crack as it hardens, and so resists the dye completely.

In Japan, either rice paste or a paste made from rice starch is the most easily available resist. The Japanese have developed a number of techniques for decorating silks and cottons, which are used to make screens, cloths and **kimonos**. On Okinawa, one of Japan's islands, a very special technique, called *bingata*, was developed. Rice paste was **stencilled** on to the cloth to give delicate patterns of flowers, birds and trees.

In parts of China, people made blue and white patterns on coarse cloth, using a bean curd resist. The resist dried in the sun and could be rubbed off easily.

The people of the Ivory Coast, in West Africa, smear cloth with a paste made from rice starch. They use a comb to scrape patterns into the wet paste.

▲ *The craftspeople of Nigeria in Africa make big bold patterns using flour paste to resist the dye.*

▼ *This fabric from India has been prepared with paste and is ready to go into the dye bath.*

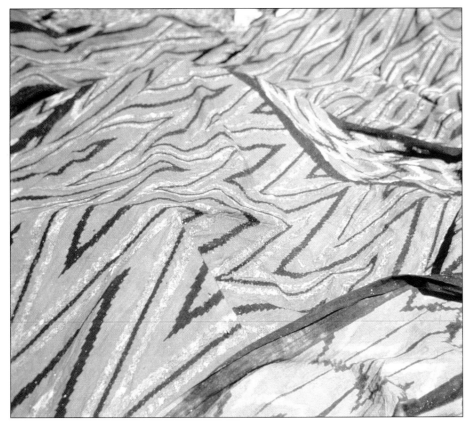

▼ *Colourful batik fabrics which will be made up into turbans and dresses.*

STEP-BY-STEP BATIK

Dye your own picture or pattern into cloth using batik. Either cover the whole area with wax and scrape it away from the parts you want in colour; or put wax only on the parts you want to stay white. Design your picture on a piece of paper, then follow these instructions.

TURN TO PAGES 22-5 FOR IDEAS ABOUT USING YOUR BATIK.

1 Dampen a piece of cloth. Pull it over a wooden frame and fix it with pins or staples. It will shrink as it dries, giving a tight surface to work on.

2 Put some batik wax or candle wax in a tin can and stand it in a saucepan of water. Make sure the water does not come more than halfway up the side of the can. Put the pan on a low heat on a ring, so that the wax melts. **Ask an adult to help you do this**.

3 Using a stiff-haired brush (such as a household painting brush), paint the melted wax on to the cloth. Coat both sides. Leave it to dry.

4 Scratch a pattern or picture into the wax. You can use all kinds of tools to do this: for example, a fork, a darning needle or a screwdriver. Turn the frame over. Make sure the wax is scraped away in the same places back and front. Remember the dye will colour the areas where you have scraped off the wax.

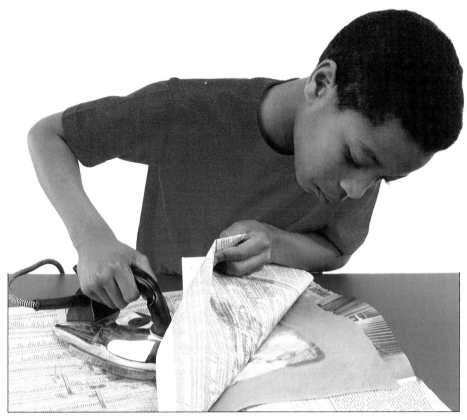

5 Now dye the cloth. Turn to pages 18-19 for information about how to do this.

6 When the cloth is dyed and dry, remove the wax. Scrape off as much as you can with a table knife.

7 Put the cloth between layers of newspaper. Press a warm iron over the top of the paper. The heat will melt the wax and the newspaper will soak it up. To get all the wax out you will have to change the layers of newspaper several times. **Ask an adult to help you use the iron**.

8 Wash the cloth several times in hot, soapy water. Rinse well, dry and give the cloth a good iron.

MORE BATIK IDEAS

USING WAX CRAYONS

1 Find an old egg poacher. Put small pieces of broken wax crayons in each holder, putting a different colour in each.

2 Half-fill the pan with water and put it on a low heat on the ring. **Remember to ask an adult to help you do this. Be careful not to let the pan boil dry**.

3 Using stiff-haired brushes, one for each colour, paint the melted wax on to the fabric. If it is hot, it will stain the fabric the colour of the crayons.

4 Brush a cold-water dye of a different colour all over the fabric. It will fill in the background.

5 Iron off the wax between layers of newspaper. Wash the cloth in soapy water, rinse and iron.

USING CANDLES

1 Prepare a fabric frame as shown on page 8.

2 Light an ordinary household candle. When it is burning well, carefully drip wax over your fabric. Experiment with trailing small drops in stripes or spirals. **Ask an adult to help you. Take care not to burn your hand. Make sure you blow the candle out properly afterwards.**

3 Dye the cloth following the instructions on pages 18-19. Iron off the wax between layers of newspaper.

DECORATING EGGS

1 Hard boil some eggs in a pan of water.

2 Paint patterns on the eggs using a brush dipped in melted wax. You can use wax crayons or candle wax.

3 Put the eggs in a bowl of water coloured with food dye.

Dye your eggs in a bowl of ▶ *water and food dye. Decorated eggs in a basket look pretty at Easter time.*

TIE-DYE AROUND THE WORLD

Tie-dye is still practised today all over the world. In many regions people have been using the same techniques for hundreds of years. They still use very simple, basic equipment.

Many West African peoples continue to produce tie-dyed fabrics, some for everyday wear, some for special occasions. The Yoruba people, from Nigeria, use a combination of tying, pleating and sewing. They also sew or tie objects they have found into the cloth to create unusual patterns. Using **indigo** dye, they produce wonderful, dark-blue, patterned cotton cloth. The women do the tying and the dyeing. The men **finish** the cloth by beating it until it shines.

▲ The patterns on this Nigerian cloth were made by sewing in raffia threads to resist the dye.

Tie-dyed fabric from Japan. Large patterns ▶ are built up by repeating simple motifs.

▼ Tie-dyed fabric drying in the sun in Nigeria. Craftspeople often work out of doors.

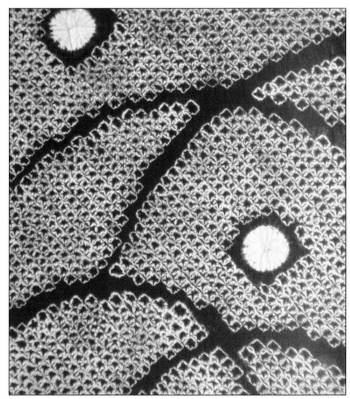

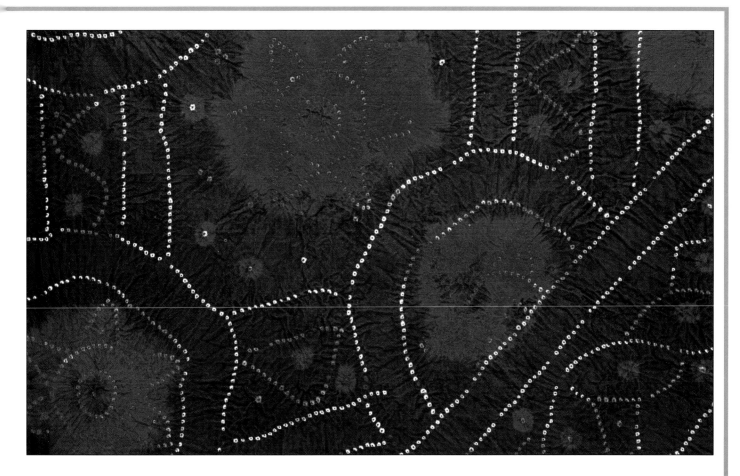

In India, tie-dyed fabrics, called *bandhani*, are made and worn in the states of Gujarat and Rajasthan. *Bandhani* are made of fine silk which is folded, dampened and pressed over a board of pins. The pins may be arranged in many different ways, and each pattern has a particular meaning. The women and children grow their nails or use a special metal thimble to pick up the tiny points of fabric off the pins. They tie the points with cotton thread.

Japanese tie-dye uses delicate colours and elaborate patterning. Large patterns are built up by repeating simple **motifs**. After the knots are untied, the fabric often remains dimpled. This makes it soft and stretchy. Clothes made from this fabric are very comfortable.

▲ Bandhani, *from India, are comfortable to wear. Dimples left by the knots have lots of 'give'.*

▼ *In Japan, tie-dyed fabric is called* shibori, *meaning tied or knotted. This piece has been untied after dyeing.*

STEP-BY-STEP TIE-DYE

Take some pieces of plain cotton fabric, about 25 cm square. Try experimenting with different ways that you can tie them up. Each way will give you a different pattern when the fabric is dyed. With practice, you will know how to plan your tying to achieve certain effects – although you can never predict exactly what will happen.

2 Tie in the pea or pebble by tightly wrapping some thin string around the cloth. Fasten it with a knot. The tighter the binding, the more the fabric will resist the dye.

3 Dye and rinse the fabric. Turn to pages 18-19 for information on how to do this.

1 Lay the cloth down flat. Place a dried pea or pebble in the centre.

4 When the fabric is dry, untie the string and iron the cloth flat.

Variations

1 Roll the fabric up and tie it at intervals.

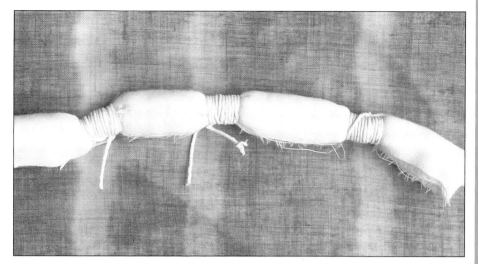

2 Place a pebble in the centre of a piece of cloth. Place smaller pebbles in a pattern over the rest of the cloth. Mark their positions with a soft pencil. Tie the pebbles into the cloth where you have marked them.

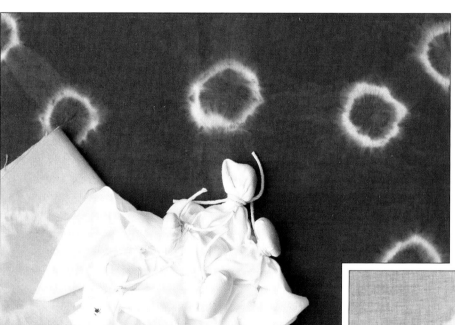

3 Tie a piece of polythene around the area you want to protect from dyeing.

There are many more ways that you can tie the fabric. Have fun experimenting. Share your ideas with your friends.

MORE TIE-DYE IDEAS

There are many ways that you can prevent dye from getting to areas of your fabric. Try using clamps, or sewing with a needle and thread. Here are some ideas to get you started.

TURN TO PAGES 22-5 FOR IDEAS ABOUT USING YOUR TIE-DYE.

1 Place a saucer in the middle of your cloth. Draw round the saucer with a soft pencil.

2 With a needle and thread, sew tacking stitches into the cloth, following the pencil line. Make two more circles of tacking stitches.

3 Tie a pebble into the centre of the cloth. Pull the threads to gather the cloth up tightly, so that the folds resist the dye. This technique, using sewing, is called tritik.

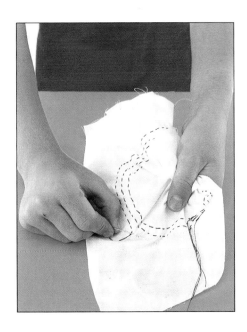

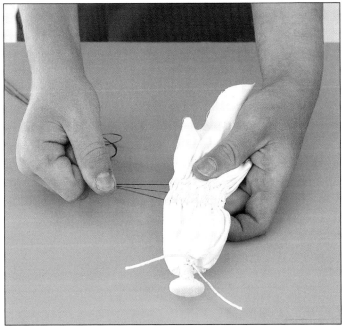

4 Turn to pages 18-19 for instructions on dyeing and rinsing.

OTHER IDEAS

1 Fold the cloth in four, then bind it with string.

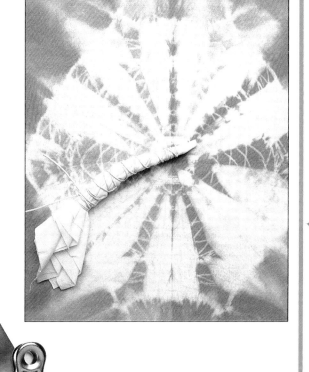

2 Fold the cloth like a concertina. Iron in the folds and clamp the cloth top and bottom using bulldog clips.

USING DYES

You can buy dyes that are ready to use straight from the packet. Cold-water dyes made by Dylon are a good, cheap choice. You can buy them from chemists, department stores and ironmongers. They are easy to use and will not melt the wax on your batiks. Different dyes are prepared in different ways. Always follow the instructions on the packet. Here are some guidelines to help you.

1 Put on rubber gloves and an overall. Dyes stain everything that they come into contact with.

2 Mix the dye powder with some hot water. **Ask an adult to help you do this**.

3 Add a tablespoon of salt. Salt helps the cloth to take the dye. You may also want to add special cold dye fixer.

4 Put the dye in a large plastic bowl or tray. Add cold water. Stir very thoroughly with a wooden spoon.

5 Damp the fabric before you put it into the dye bowl. This helps the dye to soak into the fibres.

6 Leave the fabric in the dye bowl for one hour. Stir gently every now and then, to make sure the dye colours the fabric evenly.

7 Take the fabric out of the dye. Rinse really well in the sink, changing the water three or four times to get rid of all the extra dye.

8 Hang the dyed cloth out to dry. Then remove the wax or string resist. With tie-dye, you can remove the string when the cloth is wet if you wish, but the dye may run.

9 You can also paint dye on to your cloth with a brush. This works well if you are making a batik on a frame.

10 If you are working on a piece that uses several colours, you will want to dye the cloth another colour. Turn to pages 20-21 for advice on this.

▼ *The soft brown colour of this fabric comes from onion skins.*

NATURAL DYES

In the past, people around the world developed dyes from parts of plants, animals, rocks and earth. These are still used today.

You can make your own dyes too. Onion skins give soft brown, orange and yellow colours. Boil the skins in a saucepan of water for twenty minutes. Put your cloth in the pan and leave for one hour. Rinse and dry. Try boiling other leaves, roots and stems of plants. You will need to experiment to get the range of colours you need.

PROJECTS

People all over the world use batik and tie-dye to make fabric for special clothes and other objects. There are lots of things that you can make, too.

DYEING A T-SHIRT

1 You need a plain white or light-coloured T-shirt or vest. Find the label and make sure that it is made of cotton. Cotton takes the colour well from cold-water dyes and will produce the best results.

2 If you are using a new T-shirt, wash it to get rid of the finish. The finish prevents the fabric from taking the dye.

3 Plan your batik or tie-dye design. Look at the chapters in this book to plan which technique to use, how to get the colours you want, and the number of dye baths you will need. Make some working drawings to help you.

▲ *Plan a design around the neck and sleeves only, or in bands across the top and bottom of the T-shirt.*

4 Here are some ideas. You could make a T-shirt with the design just on the front, on the sleeves, or all over.

Remember: your T-shirt must be washed separately from other clothes. Some of the dye may run in the wash and stain other clothes.

Make a wide border round ▶ *the neckline and scatter smaller patterns over the body of the T-shirt.*

Cover the front, back and ▲ *sleeves with small circles.*

▼ *Make a big circular pattern to cover the front.*

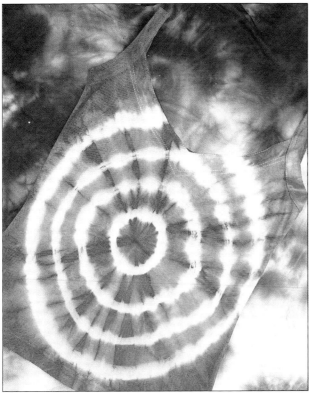

MORE PROJECTS

Decide what you are going to make and dye a piece of fabric, designing a picture or pattern to the size you want. Or, you may have made a piece of batik or tie-dye and wish to turn it into something useful.

In either case, you will need to make sure that the edges of the fabric do not **fray** by sewing a hem.

MAKING A HANDKERCHIEF, NAPKIN OR SCARF

1 Turn the fabric over so that the wrong side is uppermost.

2 Turn over 5 mm of fabric along one edge. Iron it flat so that it stays turned over.

3 Turn over another 5 mm. Now the cut edge of the fabric is hidden in the fold. Iron or pin down.

4 Thread a needle with fine sewing cotton, using a colour that matches the background colour of your fabric.

5 Catch a bit of the hem down with a tiny stitch, as invisibly as you can. Make one of these stitches every 5 mm.

6 Do the same on all four sides of the cloth.

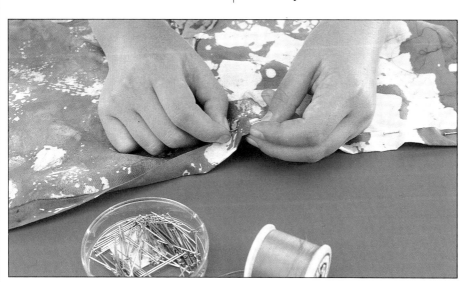

MAKING A WALL-HANGING

1 Think about where you are going to display your wall-hanging and decide what size it needs to be. Also decide what colours would look good. Design and dye your piece of fabric.

2 Hem the sides only, following the instructions opposite.

3 To hang the piece, you will need two **dowelling** rods slightly wider than your wall-hanging, to go at the top and bottom. **Ask an adult to cut the rods to the correct length**.

4 Make sockets to hold the rods. To do this, make a hem as before but the second turn should be 5 cm deep, rather than 5 mm. Insert the rods.

5 Now make a hanging thread. Cut a piece of thin string, about ten times the length of the dowelling. Dip it in one of the dye baths you used for your hanging, and leave to dry.

6 Fold the string in half, half again, half again and half again. Bind it at intervals. Dye it in another dye bath you used for your hanging.

7 When it is dry, cut the string into three equal parts, and plait it. Attach the plait to the top rod and hang on the wall.

THE GALLERY

Look at the pictures on this page. They have been chosen to give you a starting point for ideas for your batik and tie-dye designs.

▼ *Straight tree trunks.*

▲ *A painting by Jackson Pollock.*

Start to make your own collection. Choose things with shapes, colours or patterns that you really enjoy looking at. Collect shells and pebbles, sweet wrappers, pieces of driftwood or scraps of broken china. Use paper and crayons to make rubbings of natural objects, such as tree bark, or manufactured items, such as manhole covers. Cut out pictures from magazines, buy postcards and take photographs yourself.

Display your collection on a notice-board. Start making a scrap book and find a shelf or window sill where you can display your different objects.

▲ Broken tiles.

◀ Giraffe
markings.

▲ Fir cones.

◀ Umbrellas.

A peacock feather. ▶

▼ Sand patterns.

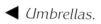

DEVELOPING DESIGN IDEAS

Use your collection of pictures, scraps and objects to develop design ideas. One item can suggest many different ideas. For instance, choose a three-dimensional object (something that has height, width and depth), such as this shell. The shell has shape, pattern and colour, but you do not need to use all of this in your design. Instead, select some aspects of the shell and develop them.

1 Look at the shell from a number of different angles and make some quick drawings to record what you see.

2 Looking down on the top of the shell might make you think of tie-dyeing a piece of fabric by rolling it up and tying it at intervals.

3 From the side the shell has a very simple shape. It looks a bit like a brush mark. Try to copy the shape on a sheet of paper, using a stiff brush dipped in hot wax. Try making patterns by arranging the shapes in different ways. Brush the paper over with coloured ink. The wax will resist the ink and show you how the design might look on fabric.

4 Look at the pattern on the shell's surface. Hold the shell in one hand and draw the part of the pattern you can see. Then turn the shell round and draw the part of the pattern you can see now. Keep doing this until you have drawn the pattern all the way round. Use the whole of the pattern for your design or choose a part of it and enlarge it.

5 Look at the colours of the shell. You might decide to dye your fabric in the same colours. Or you might decide to choose other colours for your work.

GLOSSARY

Archaeologists People who find out what happened in the past by studying ancient remains.

Brittle Easily cracked.

Designers People who work out the shape and style of an object or decoration. Their ideas are used in making the finished product.

Dowelling Thin wooden rods.

Dyes Liquid substances that are used to colour fabric or other materials.

Fabric Cloth.

Flexible Able to bend without breaking or cracking.

Finish To put a special surface on a piece of cloth, to change the way it looks, feels or behaves.

Fray To wear away or come undone at the edges.

Indigo A natural dye that comes from a plant. It gives a rich purply-blue colour.

Kimonos Long, loose robes worn in Japan.

Motifs Shapes that are repeated to make a pattern.

Primary colours The colours red, blue and yellow, from which all other colours can be made.

Resist Any kind of coating that is used to stop dye getting to certain parts of a piece of cloth.

Starch A kind of sticky sugar found in many plants, particularly rice and other cereals.

Stencilled Applied using a stencil. This is a sheet of stiff paper in which holes have been cut in the shape of a design. The stencil is laid on the surface to be decorated. Dye or paint is wiped over it to reproduce the design through the holes.

Techniques Methods or skills.

Textiles All kinds of fabric, or the threads used to make fabric.

Tjanting A batik tool. Wax is dribbled through a thin nozzle on to the cloth.

Tradition A custom that has been practised over many years, by one generation of people after another.

FURTHER INFORMATION

BOOKS TO READ

Lancaster, John *Fabric Crafts* (Franklin Watts, 1991)
O'Reilly, Susie *Textiles* (Wayland, 1991)
Singer, Margo and Spyrou, Mary *Textile Art, Multicultural Traditions* (A & C Black, 1989)

PLACES TO VISIT

Britain
The Museum of Mankind
6 Burlington Gardens
London
W1X 2EX

The Victoria and Albert
    Museum
Cromwell Road
South Kensington
London
SW7 2RL

Australia
Victoria State Craft
    Collection
Meat Market Craft Centre
Courtney Street North
Victoria 3051

Canada
Montreal Museum of Fine
    Arts
1379 Sherbrooke St West
Montreal
Quebec H3B 3E1

Royal Ontario Museum
100 Queen's Park
Toronto
Ontario
M5S 2C6

For further information about arts and crafts, contact the following organizations:

The Crafts Council
44A Pentonville Road
London
N1 9BY
UK

Crafts Council of New
    Zealand
22 The Terrace
Wellington
PO Box 498
Wellington Island
New Zealand

If you want to find out more about dyes, Dylon runs an information service. Write, enclosing a stamped addressed envelope, to:
Annette Stevens
Consumer Advice
Dylon International Limited
London SE26 5HD
Tel: 081 650 4801

INDEX

ACKNOWLEDGEMENTS

The publishers would like to thank the following for allowing their photographs to be reproduced: Bridgeman Art Library 26 right; Bruce Coleman Limited 26 left (G. McCarthy), 27 top left (J. and D. Bartlett); Eye Ubiquitous title page (J. Highet), 4 top (J. Dwyer), 4 bottom (J. Highet), 7 top and bottom right (J. Highet), 7 bottom left (L. Goffin), 12 right, 13 top (P. Seheult), 13 bottom, 27 top centre; Hutchison Library 6 right, 12 top left (J. Highet), 12 bottom left (V. and A. Wilkins); Panos Pictures 6 left; Tony Stone Worldwide 27 top and bottom right (L. Burgess); Zefa 27 bottom left, centre (G. Kalt). All other photographs, including cover, were supplied by Zul Mukhida. Logo artwork was supplied by John Yates.

The painting *Yellow, Grey, Black* by Jackson Pollock appears by kind permission of the copyright holders: © 1992 The Pollock-Krasner Foundation/ARS N.Y.

The publishers would like to thank the following schools for allowing pupils' work to appear in the photographs: Cumnor House School, Danehill, Sussex 5 (parrot picture), 23 (T-shirts top and bottom right), 24 (batik fabric); Surrey Square Junior School, Southwark 5 (patchwork quilt); Yearbury Primary School, Tuffnell Park 5 (cushion); Islington VIth Form Centre, Islington 25 (batik wall-hanging).

Thanks also to Downs Junior School, Brighton, Sussex, for allowing pupils to appear in the photographs.

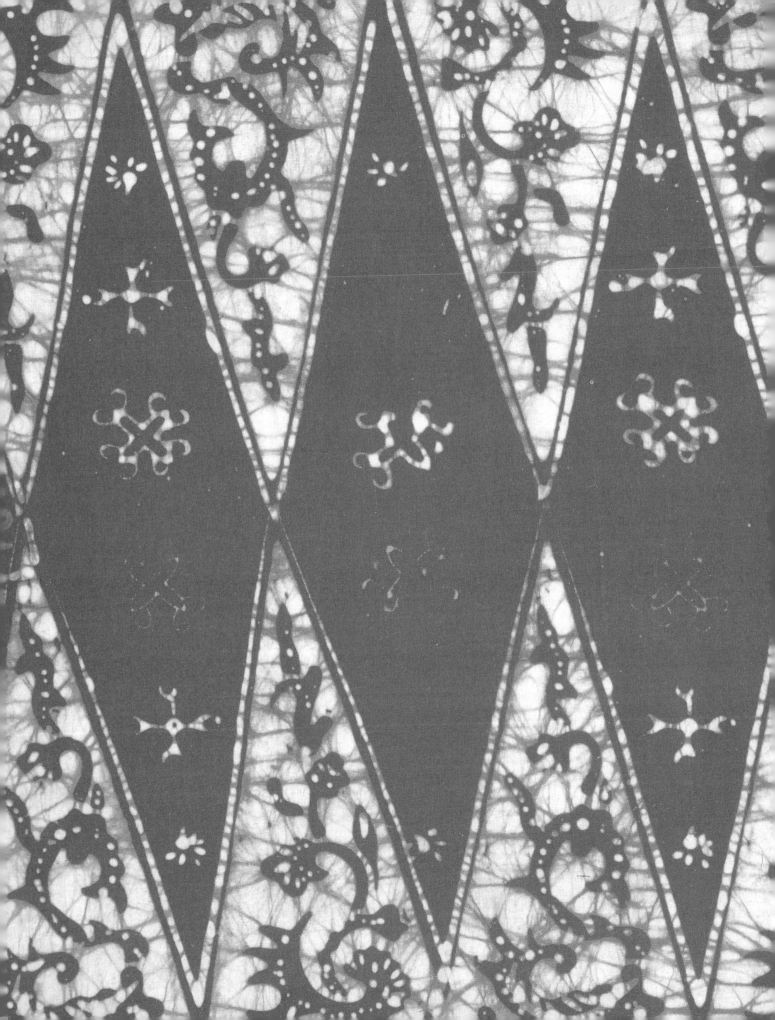